TORCRO:
and
SLAPTON LEY

ORCHARD PUBLICATIONS
2 Orchard Close, Chudleigh, Devon TQ13 0LR
Telephone: (01626) 852714

ISBN 1898964 64 5

Printed by
Hedgerow Print, Crediton, Devon EX17 1ES

i

Contents

Acknowledgements

A special thank you to Keith Chell of the Slapton Ley Field Centre, whose advice and encouragement was invaluable in producing this book and for suplying me with the pictures on the activities of the students at the centre.

I would also like to thank the head office of the Field Studies Council for their permission to use some of the diagrams in this book. They run a variety of educational courses at their Slapton Ley Field Centre for all ages. Telephone:- 01548 580466
Further information at www.field-studies-council.org

Thanks also to The Herbert Whitley Trust, who own Slapton Ley National Nature Reserve, for their help and guidance and to the Dartmouth Museum and to the Cookworthy Museum at Kingsbridge, for their help with my research.

Finally, a big thank you to the local residents and villagers who lent me their family photo albums to copy, especially Una Tester, Angela Lansdale, and David Luscombe.

For
future generations.
May there always be an unspoilt fresh water lake at
Slapton Ley National Nature Reserve for them to enjoy and admire.

The geographical formation of Slapton Ley

Coastline 100,000 years ago

In the interglacial period approximately 100,000 years ago, the coastline followed the inland shores of the present fresh water lake, known as Slapton Ley.

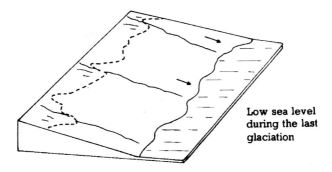

Low sea level during the last glaciation

With the onset of the last ice age, the sea level dropped as more and more of the water in the world's oceans became frozen to form the vast ice caps which covered the land as far south as London and Bristol. When the sea level was at its lowest, the coastline was twenty or thirty miles further out in the English Channel.

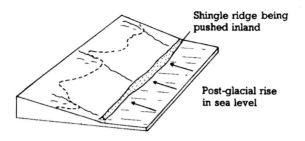

Shingle ridge being
pushed inland

Post-glacial rise
in sea level

The flint pebbles, which form most of the present shingle ridge of Slapton Sands, were eroded from chalk deposits way out in the Channel. At the end of the last Ice Age, about 10,000 – 12,000 years ago), the ice caps melted and the pebbles were pushed inland along the shoreline ahead of the rising sea level.

The shingle ridge stretched right across Start Bay from Dartmouth to Start Point, until it was finally pushed into its present position between Strete Gate and Torcross about 3,000 years ago. At this time it blocked off the estuaries of the Gara, the Start and the Stokeley rivers. This resulted in the river water building up behind the ridge, and forming the fresh water lake of Slapton Ley.

The earliest records of Torcross and the Long Sands

Map showing Henry VIII's fortifications
between Start Point and Dartmouth

The defence of coastal villages was a problem in Tudor times and it was only considered safe after the Armada was defeated and many of the marauding pirate ships had been vanquished.

Torcross was just a collection of uninhabited fishermen's huts until 1602, at which time a resident of Torcross reported that 'all was well.' This was the first recorded entry at the court of the Manor of Stokenham.

The map shows The Long Sands of Slapton fortified at each end so that cannons could be trained along the vulnerable shingle ridge. The castle at Slapton Bridge says 'not made' at the side, although other castles on the map shown as 'not made' include Fort Charles and Dartmouth Castle which were in fact already built.

However, manorial records of the 1500s do mention a drawbridge located where the present bridge stands. The Ley therefore acted as a moat to defend Slapton Village.

A brief history of the road

From a painting by W. Payne. Courtesy of Local Studies Library, Exeter.

There has been a track across Slapton Sands since Anglo Saxon days. However in times of heavy rainfall the Ley would overflow across the shingle ridge causing a breach between the fresh water and the sea, therefore making the track impassable.

In 1831 the Sands Hotel was built near the Slapton turning, on the site of the present middle car park and the granite memorial. In 1854 it was decided to build a coast road that could take coaches and horses between Dartmouth and Kingsbridge.

Welsh miners were employed to dig a tunnel under the houses at Torcross and through the cliff behind the Torcross Hotel to take the flood waters and prevent the new road being washed away (see arrow). At the same time a weir was constructed across this new outlet to control the depth of the Ley.

In 1856 the new road, as seen above passing the Sands Hotel, was opened by Governor Holdsworth of Dartmouth, whose residence was Widdicombe House on the hill above Torcross.

Local industries on and around the Ley

The open waters of the Upper Ley gave easy access to harvest the reeds which were much in demand for thatching the roofs of local dwellings.

The reeds were cut by hand in the Autumn, loaded into the boats and tied into bundles.

The bundles of reeds were stacked around the shores of the Ley, waiting to be sold to the thatchers and collected by horse and cart. The Upper Ley at that time was open water, but with increasing amounts of sediment from further upstream, it has gradually turned into a reed marsh.

The reeds had to be harvested every year, because any reeds from the previous season would have become too weak and brittle in the winter storms. Consequently all the reed beds around the Ley were cut right back annually to meet the demand for high quality by the local building industry at a time when thatched roofs were commonplace.

View of the cut reeds along the banks of the Ley by Leacliff Cottages.

Historically the reeds were kept clear in the middle of the Lower Ley for fishing. Two steam tractors were positioned on opposite shores of the Ley and a wire rope and drag was strung between the two of them so that the reeds could be pulled out by their roots to create open water. The reeds have not been harvested commercially for many years, partly because the operation is no longer economically viable, but more specifically because this would impact on the important conservation impact of the reed beds. These reed beds support a vast and diverse range of wildlife. Sadly there is a decline in such habitats nationally. The last attempt to harvest the reeds mechanically was in the early 1970s. The attempt ended in failure when the floating harvester was unable to make any headway through the dense undisturbed years of growth and because of the danger of unexploded ammunition left behind after 'Exercise Tiger' (see page 17)

The arrival of tourists and second home owners

The new coach road which crossed Slapton Sands passed the seaward side of the houses at Torcross. The road opened up the area for tourists and wealthy families from the big cities, who bought up the fishermen's houses, so that they could spend the summer in Torcross.

The hotels were also thriving as more people discovered the benefits of 'taking the waters'. The bathing machine, behind the man in smart beach attire, was wheeled down to the water's edge so that the ladies could step modestly straight into the water while dressed in their bathing costumes.

Fishing in the Ley

ROYAL SANDS HOTEL. SLAPTON. SOUTH DEVON.

Extract taken from the brochure of the Royal Sands Hotel:-
"......Of Rudd and Perch, there must be literally millions in the Ley. However it is Pike that claim the attention of most Slapton Anglers - Slapton Ley may justly be called a Pike Angler's Paradise and has yielded many a 20 pounder".

Boats were kept around the shores for the use of the locals and visitors alike. Crab pots were not used in the Ley. The photographer got carried away with his artistic props.

This boat house was built on the shore just to the north of Stokeley Bay close to the present day farm shop.

For many years Wing Commander W.C. Venmore from Torcross managed the fishing on the Ley. After his death in 1967, Slapton Ley Field Centre took control — by then fishing was only carried out from the boats kept by Slapton Bridge, and all fish caught had to be returned to the water.

Agriculture on the shores of the Ley

Farmers could graze their cattle right to the edge of the Ley.

Domestic geese also grazed the banks of the Ley. Seen here on the site now occupied by the road side pay and display car park. They were attended by local girls who made sure they did not wander off to join the visiting wild flocks.

The measured nautical mile

'Philips Ship Building Yard' in Dartmouth erected four posts with triangles on the tops, one nautical mile (6,080feet) apart. Two on the foreshore and two others on the inland side of the Ley. They were used to test boat instruments logs for accuracy.

One of the posts can be seen on the right of the photo, next to an old boiler which was used to tar the local fishermen's nets and ropes.

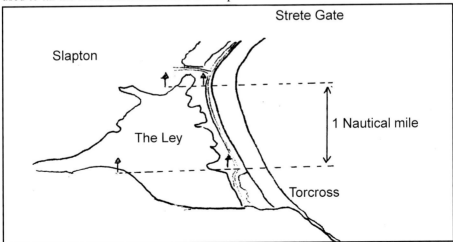

The boats travelling across Start Bay would line up the post on the foreshore with the inland post. When the two appeared directly one above the other, this marked the start of their run and finish when the other pair appeared in line,

The post with its triangular top can be seen on the foreshore at the northern end of the measured nautical mile, close to the Royal Sands Hotel. The other one of this pair was positioned in the field of South Ground Farm.

The southern inland post (circled) was positioned in the field above houses at Torcross.

A Sporting Estate for sale!

This etching of the 1800s shows the Boxing Day shoot on Slapton Ley with the landlord's party in the boats and his tenants allowed around the shores with their muzzle loading guns. In 1898 the Stokeley Estate, including the Ley was sold off to pay death duties. It was advertised as a Residential and Sporting estate. The sales catalogue boasted *"the bag in Coots alone, for one day, has numbered 1,500."*

SLAPTON LEY

IS A LARGE FRESH WATER LAKE.

IT AFFORDS THE BEST OF SHOOTING AND FISHING.

SHOOTING. The Shooting is both varied and good. The natural contour of the land, the nature of the soil, and the undulating and secluded Plantations, intersected as they are by small streams of water, favour, in a remarkable degree, the successful Breeding and Rearing of all kinds of Winged and Ground Game; while the Ley, being the resort of an enormous number of Wild Fowl, including Wild Duck, Tufted Duck, Teal, Widgeon, Mallard, Coot, Moor Hen, Water Rail and Snipe, the sport in this direction is practically unlimited. As an instance of this, it may be pointed out that the bag in Coots alone for one day has numbered some 1,500. The Ley is also the favourite resort of the Bittern and other rare species of Wild Fowl.

FISHING. The Ley affords probably the best Pike Fishing that can be obtained. Baskets of 40 lbs. and upwards have frequently been recorded, one catch in 4 hours reaching 92½ lbs., and consisting of 18 Fish, or an average of 5 lbs. each. Some of the largest Pike caught within the last few years have scaled 29½ lbs., 24 lbs., 20½ lbs., and hundreds approaching that weight. The Perch and Rudd Fishing is equally good, many baskets reaching 400 and upwards. In addition to the above, the Ley also abounds with Eels.

Herbert Whitley (benefactor of Slapton Ley)

Herbert Whitley was an eccentric millionaire who worked most days in an open necked shirt, a well patched jacket, scruffy trousers and string tied sandals.

He and his brother William bred pedigree animals on their farms in and around Paignton. This lead to Herbert's dream to breed exotic animals. He realized this dream in the early 1920s when he founded Paignton Zoo.

In 1921 he heard that Slapton Ley was under threat of being drained and the land reclaimed so that a holiday resort could be built. It was also rumoured that an earlier plan to direct a railway line (some of it electrified) across Slapton Sands was being reconsidered. Determined to prevent this happening, Herbert purchased the estate as a wildlife sanctuary, for the price of £21,750.

Most of the Stokeley Estate had been kept intact since the earlier sale in 1898 by the Newman family from Blackpool Sands. The estate consisted of Stokeley House and farm, the Upper and Lower Ley together with Slapton Woods and France Woods, the Royal Sands Hotel, and four other farms around the Ley.

In 1954 Slapton Ley was declared a Site of Special Scientific Interest (a SSSI) because it was the largest freshwater lake in the south west and because of all the special flora and fauna around its shores.

On his death in 1955 Herbert Whitley had left The Stokeley Estate, together with his properties in Paignton for the endowment of a new charitable, educational and scientific foundation to be known as the Herbert Whitley Trust.

Unfortunately his estate incurred a death duty liability of £500,000. It soon became clear to the new trustees that the income from the five farms was insufficient to support a nature reserve. The farms were disposed of in 1956, leaving the nature reserve consisting of the two Leys, France and Slapton Woods, the Line and various waterside fringes, totaling some 460 acres.

In 1959 Slapton Ley Field Centre was established by the Field Studies Council. A year later the Field Studies Council leased the Nature Reserve from the Whitley Trust and took over the management of the estate.

The Second World War

In November 1943 the residents of Torcross and Slapton together with the residents of Stokenham, Chillington, Frogmore, Sherford, Blackawton, East Allington and Strete were given just six weeks to vacate their homes, taking all their possessions with them. The whole area was to be taken over by American forces to prepare for the invasion of Normandy the following June.

28th April 1944 Slapton Sands was used for Exercise Tiger in preparation for the D-Day landings. Unfortunately nearly 1,000 American soldiers were killed in this exercise, most of them killed at sea when their convoy was attacked by German E-boats, but others were killed on the beach with the use of live ammunition.

After the infantry had secured the beach head and moved inland, tanks and heavy equipment were landed along Slapton Sands.

The Royal Sands Hotel was destroyed by naval gunfire and medium bombers although a popular local story is that a dog wandered into the mine field around the hotel and started a chain reaction!

The once proud Manor House Hotel at Strete Gate was also destroyed in the bombardment, and was never repaired.

The ruined hotel was levelled to the ground in recent years to create the picnic area next to the car park at the northern end of the Upper Ley.

Panoramic view of Start Bay an

ton Ley National Nature Reserve.

Monuments and memorials to the war years

In June 1954 the Monument was presented by the United States Army in gratitude to the people of the South Hams who had vacated their homes. In 2001 the monument became undermined by the sea , so it was dismantled and re-erected next to the middle car park.

In 1984 a Sherman tank was recovered after forty years on the sea bed and erected as a memorial to those who gave their lives in Exercise Tiger.

Recovery of the Sherman tank from the sea bed in 1984

Divers first attached floatation bags to the tank to raise it from the seabed so that it could be towed into the shallows where it could be dragged out of the water using steel ropes and a land based pulley.

Local hotelier Ken Small (seen here with his wife Ann) was the man responsible for bringing the tank ashore. He was to spend the rest of his life telling the story of the sacrifices of those who took part in Exercise Tiger. Sadly he died just weeks before the 60th anniversary of that tragic event.

The tracks of the tank were locked solid as it was dragged up the beach, but as soon as it touched the concrete slipway they started to turn as if they had only just left the factory.

Four of the surviving veterans of Exercise Tiger came over from the United States to mark the 60th Anniversary and to tell their harrowing stories to the world's media.
From left to right are Richard Ferguson, Steven Sadlon, William Hicks and Louis Seibel.

Storm damage

In 1951 after a winter of south easterly storms, the beach level dropped so low that the shingle was washed away beneath the promenade.

In 1978 The sea once more battered the village of Torcross with two violent storms that unfortunately coincided with spring tides. The wall buit in 1954 held, but severe erosion took place where the wall ended.

The storm of 1978 created waves so big that they reached roof height and flowed a metre deep down the alleyways between the houses. The waves also washed right over the A379 road and into the Ley, making the road impassable.

Once again the winds were from the south east and the beach was cut away below the unprotected houses. Four houses were lost and many others badly damaged. To prevent this happening again a new sea wall was built — thanks to the efforts of the Torcross Defence Group which at the time was led by Laurie Emberson.

Defence against the sea

A huge trench was dug to form a bank on the seaward side so that work could carry on at all tides. Steel piles were then driven twelve metres down into the shingle.

After they had been cut off level, they were then capped with concrete. Further reinforced concrete beams were formed to brace against the promenade wave return wall. Large boulders were concreted in place between the beams so that if the beach level drops again the protruding boulders will break up the force of the waves.

Sarah Rose-Price and Clare Stubbs presented bouquets to the Queen and Prince Philip when they came to open the new defences in 1981.

The storm of 11th January 2001 undermined the road just north of the Slapton turning. The local council placed large boulders in the damaged area to prevent further erosion. Unfortunately all these had to be later removed as a condition of planning approval for the new section of the road. The whole of the shingle ridge is a 'Site of Special Scientific Interest' and no foreign material can be dumped on a SSSI. Also it was feared that any hard defence would encourage extra erosion at the points where that defence ended.

The double curves of the new road were completed in the spring of 2002 and can be seen between the beach and the reed marsh of the Upper Ley just north of the Slapton turning.

The sea does not always take away the beach, it sometimes builds up the ridge with its wash over action at which time stones and shingle are deposited on the road and into the Ley behind it. In so doing the ridge has gradually moved inland with the rising sea levels since the last Ice Age.

Extremes of weather

Snow and frost are very unusual for the Nature Reserve, but in 1963 the Ley froze over. The ice was so thick that Britannia Royal Naval College cadets were able to come and hold an ice hockey tournament on it.

Residents of Torcross also enjoyed the unusual experience. However, when hot refreshments were wheeled onto the ice, the large gathering around the tea trolley caused the ice to groan dramatically and everyone scattered!

During the long hot summer of 1976 the Ley dried out leaving only muddy pools in the middle. Although some of the local lads tried to walk across, it was fairly treacherous.

Whenever there is a strong wind from the south or south-east the waves push the shingle up around the mouth of the tunnel on the beach, stopping the flow of water which drains the Ley, and the water cannot escape. If the mechanical digger cannot get around the headland, which is only just passable at low tide in calm weather, to clear the shingle away, then the water level soon rises and floods across the road.

Bird watching

Slapton Ley National Nature Reserve has been acknowledged a 'Spotlight Reserve' which means it is of national importance both in terms of breeding birds and for rare passage migrants. Bittern, marsh harriers, and cettis warblers are a few of those found on the reserve, together with the seasonal roosts of swallows and starlings, which can number tens of thousands.

View from the public bird hide overlooking Stokeley Bay and reed marsh.

Walks through the Nature Reserve

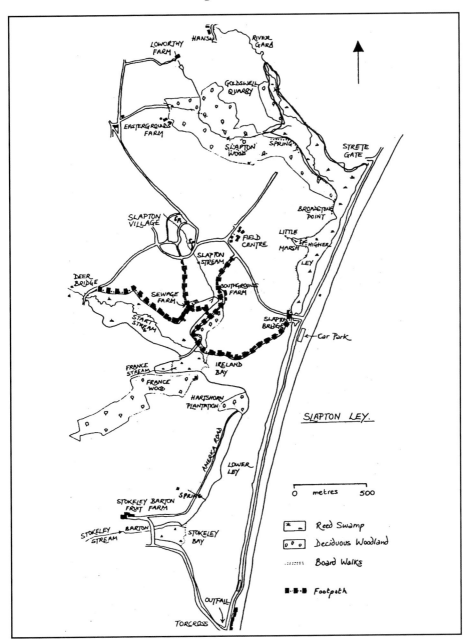

Starting at the middle car park, on Slapton Sands, walk across Slapton Bridge then turn left through the swing gate into the reserve.

33

The Nature Trail

First pause at the boat house to see what birds have been spotted recently, so that you can try to spot them too. These are recorded on a blackboard just inside the lean-to, next to the boat house.

The trail then takes you around the north shore of Ireland Bay on this fabulous family walk with interest for all.

The first landmark you come to is an old World War II machine gun bunker, left behind from the exercises preparing for D-Day.

A little further on you cross over the new viewing platform, with its superb carved hand rail. Funding for this was a joint venture between the Field Studies Council and English Nature.

The path widens and offers a lovely shady resting place where you can sit and listen to the sounds of nature without the background hum of human activities. There is a gate just opposite this site that leads to the strictly restricted area of the reserve. Even the staff of the reserve rarely enter this area, so as to encourage wildlife to settle there. Please do not be tempted to trespass here.

Soon you are offered a choice of routes:-
1.   The shortest route is past South Ground Farm and out to the Field Centre.
2.   The other two follow the board walk. The shorter of the two taking you past the sewage treatment works and back to the Slapton Village.
3.   The longer walk taking you out to Deer Bridge.

Both walks 2 and 3 take you across this lovely board walk through the marsh and the reed beds.

Walk 2 gets you to the pub quicker, but it takes you right past the new sewage treatment work. Prior to 2005 all treated sewage was discharged directly into the nature reserve, adding massively to the nutrient enrichment problems in the Ley. The treated sewage is now piped back to the coast and discharged into the sea between Torcross and Beesands.

When you reach Deer Bridge you have a choice of directions. You can either turn right towards Slapton or turn left and walk up the hill and along the lanes to Stokenham. Continue the walk down past Stokeley House and around the southern shore of the Nature Reserve.

Pause at Torcross to feed the ducks (the author — Robin Rose-Price with his grandson Euan) or visit one of the excellent tea rooms, pubs or cafes in the village. When refreshed, walk back along the coastal path to your car. By which time you will have walked over six miles in total.

Slapton Ley Field Centre

The Field Studies Council purchased this building in 1959, but did not lease the Nature Reserve from the Whitley trust until the following year. Since then many classrooms and dormitories have been added to accommodate the many visiting groups from schools, universities and adult education courses.

Students studying plant colonization on the shingle ridge.

Beach profile recordings are taken by visiting students at ten different locations along Slapton Sands, making this one of the best recorded sites for long shore drift in the country.

Pond dipping creates interest and fun for all ages and abilities. It also demonstrates the huge biodiversity of the Ley.

Another group of students study the composition of the beach from a variety of pebbles, including flint, quartz, slate and broken shells. You will also find pebbles of granite washed down from Dartmoor over the millennia.

The undisturbed woods around the reed marsh of the Upper Ley abound with wildlife and offer superb opportunities for studying different species.

41

What is the future for Slapton Ley National Nature Reserve?

Will it be destroyed by natural forces, as happened at Porlock Weir on the edge of Exmoor? At that location the shingle ridge breached in recent years and was not repaired. Since then the gap in the shingle ridge has gradually enlarged as the water races in and out with each tide.

All the original vegetation and trees up to half a mile inland have died as their roots sucked up the salt water. The area has now become a salt water marsh.

The future of the A379 coast road.

The future of the road accross the shingle ridge is a little more secure as the consultants who carried out the main study for the Slapton Line Partnership have reported that the cheapest option will be to allow any damaged section of the road to be rebuilt just inland of its present position as long as the ridge does not fully breach.
(see www.saveslaptoncoastroad.co.uk)

However, preparation has already taken place at Slapton Bridge to protect either the Upper or Lower Ley in the event of a breach affecting one or other of them. Shuttering will be dropped between the steel guide rails which have been secured to the bridge. This will form a weir and prevent salt contamination of the whole area.